BUDGIES CARE

A comprehensive guide on how to care, groom, feed, train and house budgies with tips on how to raise a happy and healthy pet

Nathan Ark

Table of contents

CHAPTER ONE

Introduction

One of the most common types of caged birds kept as pets all throughout the globe is the budgerigar, sometimes known as a parakeet. These little, bright birds have been kept as pets for more than a century, and they are adored for their happy personalities, amusing behavior, and gorgeous plumage. Loved for their bright personalities, lively behavior, and beautiful plumage. In this book, we will discuss all you need to know about the proper care of your budgie, including its physical features, housing and surroundings, feeding and nutrition, health and veterinary treatment, behavior and training, breeding and genetics, and a great deal more. This book will equip you with the information and resources you need to ensure that your feathery buddy has a long and healthy life, regardless of whether this is your first time owning a budgie or if you are an experienced bird lover.

Brief history of budgies as pets

Although budgies have been kept as pets for more than a century, their history as companions to humans dates far further back in time. Budgies found in the wild are endemic to Australia, where they have coexisted with flocks consisting of hundreds or thousands of other birds for thousands of years. But it wasn't until the late 1800s that budgies were first brought into Europe. Once there, they soon gained popularity as unusual pets because of their unique appearance.

The first known instance of breeding budgies in captivity took place in England in the 1850s. By the early 1900s, huge numbers of budgies were being grown specifically for the purpose of being purchased as pets. In the 1920s, the English Budgerigar Society Cage, which was the first cage that was created with the express purpose of housing budgerigars, was created. This contributed to the growing popularity of keeping budgerigars as pets.

There are millions of these adorable little parakeets being kept as pets in households all over the world, which contributes to the fact that budgies are now one of the most popular pet birds in the world. People like budgies because of their bubbly personalities, fun demeanors, and the stunning variety of colors and feather patterns that they display.

Physical Attributes of Budgies

In comparison to other types of parrots and parakeets, budgies are characterized by their smaller size, high level of activity, and distinctive look. The following is a list of some of the most important physical traits of budgerigars:

1. Size Budgies are relatively little birds, with an average length of around 7 inches when measured from beak to tail.

2. Color Budgies are well-known for their colorful plumage, which may be

seen in a wide variety of hues, including as blue, green, yellow, white, and even gray. There are also some Budgies that have unique patterns or mutations on their feathers, such as pied or spangle feathers.

3. Budgies have feathers that are downy and fluffy all over their body, but the feathers on their wings and tail are longer and more pointed. These feathers are specifically engineered to assist the bird in flying and navigating its natural habitat more swiftly.

4. Beak Budgies have a beak that is pointed and sharp, making it ideal for breaking open hard foods like seeds and nuts. They also utilize their beak for exploring their surroundings and maintaining their personal hygiene.

5. Budgies have zygodactyl feet, which means that they have two toes that face forward and two toes that face backward on each foot. Because of the peculiar form of their feet, they are able to sit safely and maneuver easily among the branches and toys.

In general, budgies are stunning birds that have a unique look, which is one of the reasons why so many people want to keep them as pets. Bird watchers of any age are likely to be delighted by their one-of-a-kind characteristics and vibrant plumage.

CHAPTER TWO

Housing and Environment for Budgies

Budgies need a living environment that is secure, pleasant, and conducive to their unique requirements for physical activity, social interaction, and cerebral stimulation. The following are some important things to keep in mind when it comes to the habitat and housing for budgerigars:

1. Cage Budgies need a large, open-air cage that gives them plenty of room to soar and run about. For a single budgie, a cage with dimensions of at least 18 inches in length, 18 inches in width, and 18 inches in height should be provided. This is a decent rule of thumb. It's best to have a bigger cage if you want to house numerous

budgies. The cage need to be constructed from hardy materials like metal, and it ought to contain vertical and horizontal bars for climbing and perching respectively.

2. Location: The cage has to be put in a calm, well-lit section of the house that is out of the way of any drafts, sources of direct sunlight, or vents for the central air conditioning or heating system. Budgies are sensitive to shifts in temperature and must be kept in a constant, moderate environment with the temperature ranging from 70 to 80 degrees Fahrenheit.

3. Perches and toys: In order to keep their minds and bodies busy, budgies require a variety of perches and toys to play with. In order to encourage good

foot health, perches should be constructed of natural wood or plastic that is not harmful, and they should range in diameter. Toys have to be fabricated from secure and non-toxic materials, and they ought to feature components that might be chewed on, shredded, and used for playing.

4. Food and water: On a daily basis, budgies need both fresh food and water. A dish for drinking water and a separate dish for meals should be supplied at all times. Seeds, pellets, and fresh fruits and vegetables are common components of a budgie's diet.

5. Cleaning: In order to maintain their health, budgies need a living environment that is kept clean. The

enclosure must to be cleaned on a regular basis, and at the very least once a week, new bedding ought to be given. Dishes used for food preparation and drinking water should be cleaned every day.

You may assist your budgie in flourishing and leading a life that is full of pleasure and health by providing it with a living environment that is secure, comfortable, and offers many opportunity for physical activity and cerebral stimulation.

Cage requirements and considerations

Because budgies spend a large amount of time in their cages, it is essential to provide them with a habitat that is not only safe but also pleasant and exciting. The following is a list of important criteria and concerns with regard to the budgerigar's cage:

1. The budgie should be able to freely fly, climb, and move about in the cage, thus the space should be enough for these activities. For a single budgie, a cage with dimensions of at least 18 inches in length, 18 inches in width, and 18 inches in height should be provided. This is a decent rule of thumb. It's best to have a bigger cage if you want to house numerous budgies.

2. The bars of the cage should have a tight enough gap between them to prevent the budgie from escaping or getting their head trapped between the bars. For budgies, a distance of one half an inch to one and a half eighths of

an inch is the proper spacing.

3. Construction: The crate should be constructed out of materials that are strong and non-toxic, such as aluminum. Steer clear of cages constructed of wood since they may be a breeding ground for germs and are difficult to disinfect.

4. Perches: In order to maintain good foot health and to exercise their feet, budgies need a variety of perches. In order to avoid issues with the feet, perches need to be crafted from natural wood or non-hazardous plastic, and their diameters ought to range.

5. Toys and accessories: Budgies are lively birds who are naturally inquisitive and need a significant amount of

mental stimulation. To prevent your budgie from being bored, provide a number of different toys and accessories for it to play with, including as swings, mirrors, bells, and ladders.

6. Dishes for the food and water The cage has to have separate dishes for both the food and the water. Choose bowls that are simple to clean and replenish, and position them in a spot where the budgie will have no trouble getting to them.

7. Position: The cage has to be put in a calm, well-lit location of the house that is out of the way of any drafts, sources of direct sunlight, or vents for the central air conditioning or heating system.

You can assist your budgie in flourishing and leading a life that is full of pleasure and good health by creating a living environment that is secure, comfortable, and exciting for it.

Toys and other items for stimulation

Budgies are lively and inquisitive birds that need a lot of mental stimulation in order to avoid being bored and to have a life that is both healthy and joyful. The following is a list of several toys and accessories that might assist you in keeping your budgie amused:

1. Swings: Budgies like swinging back and forth on swings, and swinging is an excellent method to give both physical and mental stimulation for your pet. Pick a swing for your budgie that is the right size for it and is constructed of

materials that aren't harmful or hazardous in any way.

2. Budgies are gregarious birds that thrive when they are in the company of other avian species. Both the illusion of having a company and the mental stimulation it provides may be provided by a mirror.

3. Budgies like making noise, therefore providing them with aural stimulation via the use of bells is an excellent idea. You should get a bell for your budgie that is the right size for it and manufactured out of materials that are safe and non-toxic.

4. Ladders: Budgies are energetic pets who like the challenge of climbing. Climbing a ladder is good for both your physical and emotional health. Choose

a ladder that is both the right size for your budgie and constructed of materials that are safe and won't harm it, like as wood or plastic.

5. Puzzle toys: Budgies are smart birds who like the challenge of trying to figure things out. A cerebral workout and a break from monotony are both benefits that may come from playing with a puzzle toy like a foraging toy.

6. Chew toys: Budgies have a natural desire to chew, and offering a safe, non-toxic chew toy may minimize harmful chewing behavior and give mental stimulation. Budgies have a natural propensity to chew.

7. Perches: Budgies need a variety of perches so that they may maintain good foot health and avoid becoming

bored. Offer perches made on a variety of materials, including natural wood and plastics that are safe for use with animals.

You may contribute to keeping your budgie cognitively busy, happy, and healthy by giving a range of toys and accessories for it to play with. Don't forget to choose out things that are the right size and are manufactured of materials that aren't harmful or hazardous.

CHAPTER THREE

Diet & Nutrition for Budgies

A nutritious food is very necessary for the overall health of your budgie. When it comes to providing your budgie with food, here are some pointers to keep in mind:

1. Pellets: You should aim to provide the majority of your budgie's food in the form of high-quality pellets. Pellets are an excellent source of vitamin, mineral, and other necessary elements and give a balanced diet.

2. Fresh fruits and veggies It is also important to provide fresh fruits and vegetables on a regular basis. Options worthy of consideration are dark, leafy greens like spinach, kale, and broccoli. Additionally worthy of consideration are

sweet potatoes, carrots, and bell peppers.

3. Seeds: Due to the large amount of fat and the low amount of important nutrients that seeds contain, they should be supplied in restricted amounts. Steer clear of diets consisting only of seeds if you want to stay healthy.

4. Sweets and treats: Sweets and treats like millet spray, dried fruit, and nuts should be fed only in moderation.

5. Water: At all times, there should be access to water that is both fresh and clean. Each day, the water should be changed to avoid the formation of germs.

6. Cuttlebone and mineral block: In order to assist preserve the health of

your budgie's beak and bones, you should supply it with cuttlebone and mineral block.

7. You should steer clear of giving your budgie any things that might potentially be harmful to it, including as chocolate, avocados, coffee, alcohol, and meals that are heavy in salt or sugar.

It is important to make sure that your budgie has access to a healthy food and that you do not overfeed it. Obesity may lead to a variety of health issues. If you have any queries or worries about the nutrition of your budgie, you should speak with a veterinarian that specializes in the health of birds.

Various kinds of foods and unique treats

The following is a list of some particular examples of foods and treats that are appropriate for budgerigars:

1. Pellets: The majority of their food should be comprised of high-quality pellets that have been created expressly for budgies. Pellets developed to provide the essential vitamins, minerals, and nutrients may be purchased from companies like Kaytee, Zupreem, and Roudybush.

2. Offer a wide range of fresh fruits and vegetables on a regular basis, such as spinach, kale, broccoli, carrots, sweet potatoes, apples, bananas, and berries. This should be done in order to keep things interesting.

3. Seeds: As a special treat, you may provide your pet with seeds such as millet spray, sunflower seeds, and pumpkin seeds in little amounts.

4. Sweets and treats: Sweets and treats, such as honey sticks, dried fruit, and nutri-berries, should be provided in moderation.

5. Cuttlebone and mineral block: Providing your pet with cuttlebone and mineral block may assist in maintaining the health of their beak and bones.

It is essential to keep in mind that the diet of a budgie should be well-rounded and include a variety of foods. You should provide your budgie with a variety of meals as well as treats to keep it from becoming bored and to make sure it is receiving all of the nutrients it needs. Do not feed your budgie any food that is heavy in salt, sugar, or fat, or that may be poisonous to birds, such as chocolate, avocados, coffee, or alcohol. These foods should be avoided at all costs. If you have any queries or worries regarding the nutrition of your budgie, you should discuss them with a veterinarian who specializes in the health of birds.

Getting a Feeding schedule

The frequency of feedings and the amount of food given to budgies might change based on their age, size, and the amount of exercise they get. The following are some general pointers to keep in mind:

1. Pellets: Provide pellets to your budgie as the primary component of its food, and provide around one to two

teaspoons of pellets on a daily basis. Keep an eye on your budgie's weight and make adjustments to the amount of food as required to avoid either obesity or poor nutrition.

2. Fresh fruits and veggies: Each day, provide a selection of fresh fruits and vegetables, and provide around one to two teaspoons of chopped or grated produce. provide a range of fruits and vegetables. In order to keep the food from going bad, fresh vegetables should be offered first thing in the morning, and any uneaten pieces should be removed after a few hours.

3. Seeds and treats: Provide seeds and treats to your students on occasion in the form of snacks or prizes, and aim to give them between one and two

teaspoons every week. As a method for encouraging good behavior, you might try giving the bird some seeds and snacks in the afternoon or early evening.

4. Water: Ensure that there is always a supply of fresh, clean water available, and ensure that it is routinely replaced and washed in order to avoid the formation of bacteria in the water dish.

It is essential that you keep an eye on your budgie's weight on a regular basis and make any necessary adjustments to their feeding schedule and the amount of food they consume. Underfeeding may result in malnutrition and stunted development, while overfeeding can lead to obesity and other health concerns. If you have any queries or concerns regarding the feeding schedule and amount of food that you should be giving your budgie, you should speak with a veterinarian that specializes in the health of birds.

Water requirements and hygiene

You should always make sure that your budgie has access to water since it is vital to its well-being. The following are some tips about the need of water and hygiene:

1. Water that is fresh and clean should be provided on a daily basis. If the water is clean and fresh, budgies will drink more of it; thus, you should replace the water every day, even if the bowl hasn't been completely empty.

2. Your budgie should drink from a clean water dish or water bottle as its source of hydration. In order to avoid getting the food contaminated, you should make sure that the water is conveniently accessible and far away from the meal.

3. Quality of the water: Drink only purified water that has been bottled or filtered, or water from the tap that has been boiled or treated with a water conditioner to eliminate any potentially hazardous contaminants.

4. Clean the water bottle and water dish on a regular basis, at least once a week, to avoid the formation of germs and maintain good hygiene. Before adding new water, wash the container well with soap and water, then sanitize

it by rinsing it many times and allowing it to dry fully on its own.

5. Be sure to keep an eye on how much water your budgie is drinking. If you find that your budgie is drinking an abnormally large amount of water or none at all, you should take it to a veterinarian who specializes in the health of birds since this might be an indication of an underlying medical condition.

6. Additives for water: You should avoid adding any vitamins or supplements to the water since doing so might encourage the development of germs and affect the flavor of the water, which can lead to a reduction in how much water you drink.

It is essential to provide your budgie clean, fresh water at all times and to exercise proper hygiene in order to forestall the development of germs that may be detrimental to your pet. By adhering to these instructions, you may assist in ensuring that your budgie maintains a healthy body and enough levels of hydration.

CHAPTER FOUR

Health and Veterinary Care for Budgies

Maintaining your budgie's good health is essential to ensuring their happiness. The following is a list of suggestions for keeping your budgie in good health and locating veterinarian treatment when it is required:

1. Routine examinations It is recommended that you see a veterinarian who specializes in avian health on a yearly basis for examinations. This may assist in the early detection of any possible health concerns, therefore ensuring that your budgie is in excellent health.

2. A person who is sick may exhibit symptoms such as fatigue, loss of

appetite, weight loss, difficulty breathing, or changes in behavior. It is important to be aware of any and all of these symptoms. If you detect any of these signs, you should get in touch with your veterinarian as soon as possible.

3. Maintaining proper hygiene in the budgie's cage includes cleaning the food and water bowls on a regular basis, giving the cage a thorough cleaning once a week, and doing additional spot cleaning as required.

4. Reducing Stress: One of the most effective ways to reduce stress is to create an atmosphere that is comfortable and calm, and to avoid making abrupt changes to one's routine or making loud sounds.

5. Provide toys, perches, and chances for flight in order to encourage frequent activity and encourage regular exercise.

6. Controlling parasites requires that you keep an eye out for any symptoms of infestation, like as mites or lice on your budgie, and seek veterinarian attention if required.

7. Care in an Emergency You should look for an emergency veterinarian who specializes in the health of birds in the event of a medical emergency.

You can help guarantee that your budgie has a long and healthy life by providing it with the proper care and attention and by bringing it to the veterinarian when it is required.

Common symptoms and health issues

The following is a list of typical health problems that might afflict budgerigars, as well as their symptoms:

1. Infections in the respiratory tract may cause a variety of symptoms, including sneezing, wheezing, nasal discharge, difficulty breathing, and a reduction in activity level.

2. Budgies may pick at their feathers for a variety of reasons, including anxiety, boredom, or even a medical condition. Loss of feathers, bald spots, and skin irritation are some of the symptoms of this condition.

3. Beak and feather disease: This viral condition may result in abnormalities of the beak and feathers, such as

overgrowth or an aberrant form. It is also possible for it to cause infections of the skin and feathers.

4. Vitamin A insufficiency is characterized by a decrease of appetite, which may lead to significant weight loss, as well as ocular issues, such as foggy or irritated eyes.

5. A diet heavy in fat is the root cause of fatty liver disease, which may lead to severe liver damage or even organ failure. Lethargy, reduced activity level, and weight loss are all symptoms of this condition.

6. Mites and lice are two types of parasites that may infest the feathers of a budgie, which can cause itching, feather picking, and skin irritation.

7. Egg-binding is a condition that manifests itself when a female budgie is unable to successfully deposit an egg. Lethargy, poor appetite, and trouble breathing are only few of the symptoms.

If you see any of these symptoms in your budgie, it is critical that you have them checked out as soon as possible by a qualified veterinarian. It is important to diagnose and treat your budgie as soon as possible so that you may increase its chances of making a full recovery and stop the disease from becoming worse.

Preventative care and maintenance

Your budgie can stay healthy and avoid common health problems with the right kind of preventative treatment and regular maintenance. Here are some tips:

1. Proper food and nutrition: Make sure to give your pet pellets, fresh fruits and vegetables, and seeds as treats on occasion, but in moderation. Steer clear of meals that are heavy in both salt and fat.

2. Maintain a clean environment by following proper hygiene procedures in the cage that your budgie resides in. These procedures should include the daily cleaning of the food and water dishes, the weekly cleaning of the cage, and spot cleaning as required.

3. Exercise: You should be sure to provide your pet with plenty of chances for exercise, such as perches and toys,

and you should also try to promote flight whenever it's feasible.

4. Budgies are sociable birds that need contact with their owners or with other budgies in order to properly socialize. Daily interaction with your budgie is essential, and if you just have one bird, you should think about obtaining it a friend.

5. Reducing Stress: One of the most effective ways to reduce stress is to create an atmosphere that is comfortable and calm, and to avoid making abrupt changes to one's routine or making loud sounds.

6. Annual checkups It is important to maintain your budgie's health and see a veterinarian who specializes in avian health on an annual basis in order to

identify any possible health problems in their early stages.

7. Controlling parasites requires that you keep an eye out for any indicators that your budgie could have them and, if required, take it to the doctor. Make use of measures for controlling parasites that are both safe and effective, as advised by your veterinarian.

If you follow these guidelines, you may assist in ensuring that your budgie continues to have a long and healthy life. It is essential to provide preventative care and routine maintenance for your budgie if you want to ensure its general health and well-being.

CHAPTER FIVE

Behavior and Training of Budgies

Budgies are smart and gregarious birds who respond well to training that emphasizes positive reinforcement, allowing them to learn new actions and tricks. The following is some advice on the behavior and training of budgerigars:

1. In order to form a strong bond with your budgie, you need spend time with it on a daily basis, during which you should chat to it, give it treats, and gradually earn its confidence. As sociable birds, budgies need contact with their owners on a regular basis.

2. Training based on positive reinforcement involves using rewards and praise to encourage desirable

actions in the animal, such as climbing onto your hand or entering their cage when commanded to do so. Always remember to train with patience and consistency.

3. Budgies are flock animals, therefore they need plenty of social contact throughout their lives. If you just have one bird, you should think about obtaining your budgie a friend to play with.

4. To avoid mental stagnation and prevent your budgie from becoming bored, it is important to provide it with toys, perches, and chances for play as well as exercise.

5. Taming and handling include easing your budgie into being handled by beginning with just a few minutes at a

time and gradually increasing the amount of time you spend with them as they get more used to it. Take care not to grip or squeeze them; instead, handle them gently.

6. Budgies are famous for their capacity to converse and imitate other noises thanks to their vocalizations. You may encourage your budgie to vocalize by chatting to it and repeating words or phrases for it to repeat after you.

7. Body language: It is important to be able to understand the body language of your budgie, such as fluffed feathers, fast breathing, or lifted wings, all of which may be signs of stress or pain.

You can assist guarantee that your budgie is content and well-behaved by providing it with an environment that is pleasant and interesting, as well as opportunities for socializing and training that makes use of positive reinforcement. You may strengthen your relationship with your budgie by training it to do tricks and behaviors that will strengthen your attachment with them. All it takes is patience and persistence.

Understanding budgie behavior and communication

Budgies are sociable creatures that interact with one another via a range of vocalizations and actions. By gaining an understanding of these behaviors and methods of communication, you can strengthen the relationship you have with your budgie and provide better care for it. The following is a list of behaviors that are prevalent among budgies, along with possible meanings for each one:

1. Body language: Budgerigars convey their feelings and intentions to one another via their use of body language. For instance, having their feathers fluffed up might mean that they are chilly or not feeling well, but having their wings elevated could mean that they are excited or aggressive.

2. Budgies are well-known for their singing, chirping, and chattering due to their unique vocalizations. They are also capable of imitating noises or phrases that they hear in their surroundings or from the people who possess them.

3. The act of using one's beak for the purpose of cleaning and grooming one's feathers is known as preening. It is an indication that one feels at ease and happy with their situation.

4. Budgies are lively creatures who get a kick out of socializing with their owners and enjoying the company of other people as they play with their toys. They may run about their enclosure by hopping or jumping, or they may fly from one perch to another.

5. Aggression is a potential trait that may be shown by budgies against other birds as well as people. Biting, puffing up of the feathers, and raising the wings are all indicators of aggressive behavior. It is essential to determine

the origin of aggressive behavior and take the necessary steps to treat it.

6. Fear: Budgies may show fear by crouching, frantically flapping their wings, or hiding from danger. In order to lessen the amount of fear your budgie experiences, it is essential to provide it with a setting that is both secure and pleasant.

You may form a deep link with your feathery buddy and create a pleasant atmosphere for them if you are able to comprehend the actions and communication styles of your budgie and react to them in an appropriate manner.

Tips for bonding and socializing with your budgie

Budgerigars are gregarious birds who take pleasure in spending time with their human companions. Here are some suggestions for improving your relationship with your budgie and exposing it to new experiences:

1. Spend some time with your budgie on a regular basis. In order to feel secure and content, pet budgies need daily connection with their human caregivers. Spend some time with them, engaging in conversation, playing with them, and providing them with snacks.

2. Budgies are often scared, therefore it is important to approach them in a quiet and collected manner. Speak in a

low voice and try not to make any jerky motions.

3. Treats are a terrific method to develop trust with your budgie and generate good connections with new experiences. Try offering your budgie their favorite treat. Treats may also be offered as incentives to trainees while they are being trained.

4. Ensure that your budgie lives in a secure and pleasant environment by providing it with all of the necessary supplies. This involves the cage being spotless, having enough of toys and perches, as well as fresh water and food.

5. Interact with them on their level to make them more comfortable. Budgerigars will feel more at ease

when you interact with them on their level. This entails lowering yourself to their eye level and presenting your hand as a perch for them to rest on.

6. Give your budgies the opportunity to engage with other birds so that they may develop their social skills. Budgies are sociable creatures who thrive when given the chance to do so. You should give some thought to obtaining your budgie a friend or acclimating it to the company of other birds in a controlled setting.

7. Learn to read their body language. Because budgies communicate only via their body language, it is essential to have an understanding of their signs. Stress or discomfort may be indicated in birds by fluffed feathers, elevated

wings, or fast breathing.

By putting these suggestions into practice, not only will you be able to forge a solid connection with your budgie, but you will also be able to provide them with an atmosphere that is conducive to their flourishing. It is important to keep in mind that creating trust and bonding takes time, so remember to be patient and persistent.

CHAPTER SIX

Basic training methods

The clever birds known as budgies may be taught to execute a wide range of behaviors and feats via proper training. The following is a list of fundamental training skills that you should teach your budgie:

1. Training your dog to touch a particular target, like as a stick or your finger, is an important part of target training. This is something that may be helpful when teaching other actions and skills. Begin by placing the target in front of your budgie and encouraging them to contact it by offering them a treat when they succeed.

2. Step-up training entails teaching your budgie to step onto your hand or

finger when instructed. This may be accomplished via step-up training. You should begin by providing your finger or hand to your budgie as a perch, and you should reward them with a treat when they walk upon it.

3. Budgies are famous for their ability to imitate voices and words due to their extensive vocal training. You may teach your budgie to pronounce certain words or phrases by constantly repeating those words or phrases and praising your budgie when it successfully imitates you.

4. Training to do tricks Budgies are capable of being taught to perform a number of tricks, including as spinning around, waving, or acting as if they are dead. To begin, simplify the task into a

series of smaller stages, and be sure to praise and thank your budgie after each successful try.

When you are teaching your budgie, it is essential to make use of methods of positive reinforcement, such as providing it with treats and complimenting it on its excellent behavior. If you want to keep your budgie calm and stress-free, you should steer clear of punishment and other forms of negative reinforcement. In addition, make sure that your training sessions are brief and regular in order to prevent your budgie from being overwhelmed. Your budgie has the potential to pick up a wide range of behaviors and skills if you are patient and consistent with your teaching.

Breeding budgies

Bird lovers may often get a sense of fulfillment from the experience of breeding budgies. The following are some of the fundamental stages involved in breeding budgies:

1. Pairing: When breeding budgies, it is important to choose a healthy and suitable pair of birds. The age at which budgies typically attain sexual maturity ranges from 8 to 12 months.

2. Nesting: You should provide a suitable box for the couple to use as a nest. Nesting material, like as shredded paper or wood shavings, should be placed within the container, and the container's dimensions should allow for the couple to enter and depart the space without difficulty.

3. Egg-laying: Female budgies will normally lay one egg every other day until the clutch is finished, and a clutch of budgie eggs will typically consist of between four and eight eggs. During this period, watch over the couple's food to make sure it's balanced and full of nutrients.

4. Incubation: The hatching process for budgie eggs normally takes between 18 and 21 days. During this period, the female will be responsible for incubating the eggs, while the male will be responsible for providing both food and protection.

5. Budgie chicks are ready to leave the nest between four and five weeks after they have been hatched on average. The parents will continue to provide

food and care for the chicks until the time comes when they are able to do it on their own.

6. Weaning: Once the chicks have reached the stage when they are able to care for themselves, you may start to wean them onto a solid diet consisting of seeds, fruits, and vegetables.

It is essential to keep in mind that successfully breeding budgies calls for a considerable investment of time, energy, and expertise. It is also essential to give some thought to the possible dangers and duties that come along with breeding, such as the need of providing care for ill or orphaned chicks. It is advised that you conduct your research and seek help from professional breeders or avian doctors if you are contemplating breeding budgies. If you are considering breeding budgies, it is recommended that you do your research.

Characteristics of male and female budgies

Both male and female budgies may be distinguished from one another based on their appearance and their behavior thanks to their unique combination of traits. The following are some examples of common differences:

Characteristics Relating to the Body:

• The cere (the region immediately above the beak) of males is often either blue or purple, while the cere of females is either brown or beige.

• Generally speaking, men have a coloration that is more vivid and brilliant than that of females, particularly around the head and the neck.

• The abdominal region of a female typically seems fuller and more rounded, while the abdominal region of a man typically has a more streamlined appearance.

Characteristics Relating to Behaviour:

• Males are often more vocal than females and may sing or whistle more frequently. This is also true of the general population.

• It's possible that females will be more hostile and territorial, particularly while they're nesting.

• Males may be more outgoing and love engaging with toys or other birds, whilst females may be more self-sufficient and prefer to spend their time alone.

It is essential to keep in mind that these features might vary from one budgie to the next and are not always accurate markers of the gender of the animal. It is highly advised that you get a DNA test carried out on your budgie by a certified veterinarian or bird expert if you want to be absolutely confident about the gender of your pet.

Breeding process and considerations

The procedure of breeding budgies is one that must first be meticulously planned out and organized. Here are some crucial considerations:

1. Pairing: When breeding budgies, it is important to choose a healthy and suitable pair of birds. When possible, try to find two birds who are of the same age but have never been bred together previously. Keeping an eye on the couple can help you determine whether or not they are a good match and whether or not they are kind to one another.

2. Nesting: You should provide a suitable box for the couple to use as a nest. Nesting material, like as shredded paper or wood shavings, should be placed within the container, and the container's dimensions should allow for the couple to enter and depart the

space without difficulty. The nesting box has to be put in an area that is free from loud sounds and other types of disruptions, as well as somewhere that is private and peaceful.

3. food: A balanced and diverse food is vital for breeding budgies. Make sure the two of them have access to a wide range of seeds, fruits, veggies, and supplements like calcium and vitamins. Egg production and the growth of healthy chicks may both benefit from a diet that is nutritionally sound.

4. Incubation: The hatching process for budgie eggs normally takes between 18 and 21 days. During this period, the female will be responsible for incubating the eggs, while the male will be responsible for providing both food

and protection. To ensure that the eggs are growing in the correct manner, it is important to keep an eye on the temperature and humidity levels in the nesting box.

5. Budgie chicks are ready to leave the nest between four and five weeks after they have been hatched on average. The parents will continue to provide food and care for the chicks until the time comes when they are able to do it on their own. Check to ensure that the nesting box has enough space to support the developing chicks and that there is a enough supply of food and water.

6. It is vital to do routine checks and provide care for the breeding couple in order to protect the birds and their

young from any potential threats to their health and wellbeing. Plan regular visits to the veterinarian and keep a close eye on the birds for any indications of disease or anxiety.

It is essential to keep in mind that successfully breeding budgies calls for a considerable investment of time, energy, and expertise. It is also essential to give some thought to the possible dangers and duties that come along with breeding, such as the need of providing care for ill or orphaned chicks. It is advised that you conduct your research and seek help from professional breeders or avian doctors if you are contemplating breeding budgies. If you are considering breeding budgies, it is recommended that you do your research.

Summary of budgies care

Budgies may make beautiful and satisfying pets, but in order for them to flourish, their owners need to provide them with a large amount of care and attention. It is crucial for their well-being to have a healthy and exciting environment provided for them, which should include a food rich in nutrients, lots of opportunities for exercise and socializing, and routine veterinarian treatment. In addition, having a better grasp of their mannerisms, requirements for communication, and training will help you develop a closer relationship with your budgie.

It is essential to keep in mind that having a budgie as a pet is a commitment for the long term, since these birds may live for up to ten to fifteen years or even more. Because of this, before you welcome one into your house, it is essential to give great consideration to the obligations and resources that are required for its care.

In general, when given the right amount of care and attention, budgies have the potential to become loving and amusing pets that also provide their owners pleasure and friendship.

Made in United States
North Haven, CT
14 May 2023

36579258R00037